Understanding Self-Discipline

A Comprehensive Guide To Achieve Unbreakable Self-Discipline With The Most Important Daily Habits For Self-Discipline, Self Esteem & Self Confidence

Written By

James Foster

© **Copyright 2021 - All rights reserved.**

The content contained within this book may not be reproduced, duplicated or transmitted without direct written permission from the author or the publisher.

Under no circumstances will any blame or legal responsibility be held against the publisher, or author, for any damages, reparation, or monetary loss due to the information contained within this book. Either directly or indirectly.

Legal Notice:

This book is copyright protected. This book is only for personal use. You cannot amend, distribute, sell, use, quote or paraphrase any part, or the content within this book, without the consent of the author or publisher.

Disclaimer Notice:

Please note the information contained within this document is for educational and entertainment purposes only. All effort has been executed to present accurate, up to date, and reliable, complete information. No warranties of any kind are declared or implied. Readers acknowledge that the author is not engaging in the rendering of legal, financial, medical or professional advice. The content within this book has been derived from various sources. Please consult a licensed professional before attempting any techniques outlined in this book.

By reading this document, the reader agrees that under no circumstances is the author responsible for any losses, direct or indirect, which are incurred as a result of the use of information contained within this document, including, but not limited to, — errors, omissions, or inaccuracies.

Table of Contents

INTRODUCTION 7

How Gender Prejudices Damage Relationships for Highly Sensitive Men (Hsm) 11

Additional Damage to HSWS and HSMS Alike 21

Good Parents Who Feel Like They Are Bad Ones 29

Calming Your Sense and Coping with Pressure 47

Hearing 49

Smelling 61

Creating a Peaceful Work Environment 71

More Happiness Even With Less Money 79

How to Reduce Stress at Work 83

Becoming self-employed 93

CONCLUSION 95

INTRODUCTION

Thank you for purchasing this book!

It is crucial for you to be patient when telling people to make adjustments when you feel overwhelmed, and not criticize anyone who likes unnecessary stimulation.

It's also helpful to have a prepared statement when you query someone for what you need. For starters, if you're requesting someone to be louder, try to develop a good relationship with the person before calling for or contacting them to create less noise with your question. Upon demonstrating to the other party that you have a reaction to the noise, tell the person that you would like to make sure that your question keeps them happy and not uncomfortable. In this book you'll learn that:

- Being a highly sensitive person is an advantage to use as a social skill.

- High sensitivity is a capacity that must be defended in order not to be a victim or to get abused by bad people.

- Being a Highly sensitive person is an advantage, not a vulnerability.

- Empathy is not a defect, it is an advantage.

HSPs have a greater feeling of pain than non-HSPs and many have indicated that when they encounter physical pain they examine instinctively what causes the problem and seek to relieve the discomfort. In general, non-HSPs can withstand greater pain. A non-HSP friend told me he had fractured his foot but had been able to ignore the agony for more than a month, even as he was employed as a carpenter. The stoicism of HSPs doesn't work.

You need to strike a balance between generating too much stimulus, causing anxiety, and too little stimuli, resulting in boredom. For example, if you consider the pressure of audiences too intense in movie theaters, you can choose to watch a movie at non-peak hours (such as the weekday matinees). You can always rent a movie, though some HSPs have recorded very daunting attempts to pick a peaceful film in the often-hectic atmosphere of most video stores. Before dinner rush, you can go to the restaurants too. Most restaurants have an early bird deal that will allow you to enjoy both a more comfortable and cheaper dining.

High sensitivity is an innate ability to perceive what comes to HSPs in a very deep, subtle way across our senses. It's not that our eyes and ears are smarter so we figure out more cautiously what goes in. We like to study, analyze, think. Not necessarily conscious of that processing. We may be mindful of thinking (or "ruminating" or "worrying," depending on the mood we're in and the problem we're grappling with), however, more often than not, that occurs without being conscious. We are therefore very intuitive because we tend to know how things turned out to be the way they are and how they play out, but without understanding how we do all of that.

We are also excellent at using subtle signals to figure out what's going on with those that can't communicate through words— animals, insects, children, unconscious pieces of humans, the ill (bodies don't use words), strangers trying to communicate with us, historical people long dead (from our interpretation of their biographies). HSPs also have close links with our own unconscious, as shown by our vivid visions. HSPs will create, through exposure to our desires and body conditions, not only reverence for the unconscious but a wise modesty regarding motives, understanding how much of what people do is triggered by unconscious urges.

Enjoy your reading!

How Gender Prejudices Damage Relationships for Highly Sensitive Men (Hsm)

Understanding HSMs is more complicated than learning HSWs. There are as many men as women born highly reactive, but in the HSP Self-Test, adult women score better, no matter how I try to remove sex-based products. Keeping in mind our society, I'm sure there's no way to compose a self-test of responsiveness that men can respond to without the intervention of a conscious or unconscious fear of being treated as unmanly. And I realize now that I am writing mainly to people who are unscarred enough to tolerate their vulnerability without becoming aggressive, or so responsive that they cannot deny it. As a consequence, most of you don't think of yourself as "typical men," which can be really positive for your partnerships. Yet, for the other gender and your own, it is still a cause of much of your troubles.

Feeling like an unaccomplished man

"He is a true man"— somehow you're going to have to show that you are, or you're going to be in serious trouble. That is the responsibility of people in this society, and much of the anxiety and need to show arises in boyhood, where patriarchy more broadly determines the actions of the perfect man. A "real man" would be rugged and calm at that age— that is, have no profound thoughts that don't appeal to the crowd. He can be unpredictable, not reactive but also recklessly impulsive. He should be intensely competitive and be effective, particularly in team sports. Without having others or revealing some weakness, he can be outgoing— that is, not even personal.

He never cries and displays emotions seldom, particularly not terror, shame or remorse. He is not, in short, really responsive. So by this reasoning, a highly reactive individual is not a "real man." William Pollack, Harvard psychology so True Boys author, has spent twenty years in our society researching people. He pointed out that male babies generally tend to be more vocal in terms of feeling than females at conception. But the rest of it is gone by high school, due to a gender straitjacket imposed by what he called the Child Code. Boys and adults, according to the law, do not show their emotions in the first instance.

This code limits not just boys, "but everyone involved, diminishing us all as human beings and ultimately rendering us outsiders to ourselves and each other." Spencer Koffman, a San Francisco psychotherapist and HSM writer for the HSP blog, Comfort Zone, explains his own encounter with the Boy Code: boys are enrolled in "gender bootcamp" at an early age, where they are trained to be gender bootcamps. From first grade comes one of my first impressions of this indoctrination. I drop off the gymnasium-jungle. I wasn't badly injured, but I was weeping from the pain of the crash. Every child and teacher's uniform response was not to comfort me but to find out boys are not crying.

This was the first and last time I wept at high. I was in school to become a "baby boy." I don't like to say that only HSMs are struggling from the Boy Code, but HSMs are facing up to it a lot harder. You are particularly influenced by your relationships with women, who carry home the biases of the society in hurtful ways that they seem ignorant of, such as accepting you as a friend but not seeing you as sexually attractive. You should still remain as afraid about the other gender as you are, but your "love-shyness" has more severe implications.

Shying away from love

Love-shyness is a concept invented by sociologist Brian Gilmartin, who has researched the limited yet troubling group of heterosexual people who have been too nervous to start or marry a committed sexual partnership while deeply wanting to. When you're love-shy you're only waiting to be romantically discarded, mostly because of your vulnerability.

But by this description most HSMs aren't love-shy, most really love-shy people are HSMs. And I think love-shyness creates an intense image of what most HSMs, to a lesser degree, fear or witness.

For example, the word may also refer to other HSWs, who both crave and fear the affection of men as intensely as love-shy men want love from women.

For either gender, love-shyness is a direct product of misogyny, operating with unique toxicity on HSPs, with our extra motives to avoid being treated as not a "real man" or "real woman." However, love-shyness is a more damaging problem for HSMs, as in romantic matters, people usually are expected to make the first step in this society. It is now more appropriate for women to display concern first, but it is also anticipated that you, as a male, should then react aggressively and assume responsibilities. A woman can delay, and "play hard to get," but that leeway is not granted to you. And what happens to your clear inherent inclination as an HSM to pause to search before you move, to see whether you like the girl you are meeting and if she's going to like you? You have to jump when you strive for a manly presence implies you have to overcome your own rage.

If you can't, you'll still be left without a friend.

Gilmartin questioned 300 love-shy people between the ages of 19 and 50 and even contrasted the younger men with the older ones — still virgins at 35 years of age. He also met 200 college people who hadn't been nervous around sex. The love-shy people have far more miserable childhoods than the non-love-shy ones and more of the older groups than the younger.

Yet most love-shy people often mentioned the various physical sensitivities that should be common for all HSPs — allergies, a rapid knee-jerk reaction, and oddly disturbed by fur, bites of insects, excessively hot or cold weather, shorter winter days, harsh sunshine, discomfort, and abrupt or irritating noises, like chalk grating on a blackboard.

The mixture of miserable childhoods and vulnerability had produced their extreme shyness in affection.

Absent and dismissive father revisited for HSMs

Sensitive boys undoubtedly endure much more from their fathers' neglect or ignorance than from non-HSMs. Not only do fathers teach boys how to live in the community, but also how to treat emotions in this society effectively as adults. A boy born by his mother alone will lack this support.

This has been written on the detrimental impact of the lack of engaged fathers on young people and the much greater absence of male peers, who often battle with young men, seeking to hold them down. Male elders are treated as traitors who, for example, send young people off to wars they will not battle on their own and refuse to ensure that on their return these soldiers are honored and cured. You may also believe, as an HSM, that you don't get more respect from older adults, for being able to stick to the Boy Code as well. You may not even think you're a member of the elite male community that everybody else admires

The complexities created by a sensitive boy when he sympathizes with his mother

Seeing the harm done by men to women, and likely harm done by your own parents, you might have felt a profound rift in your loyalties, and tremendous sympathy particularly towards your own mother. It could have been applied to all people because you perceived them as being abused by strong guys like you. Yet obviously this compassion will alienate you from your own group. In a way, you'll feel a thief in the gender wars— and wind up being respected by neither party. This impression may be reinforced by detecting slight signals that your mother might have valued you as a confidant or friend, yet again, not as a "true man"— remember the studies into" shy "sons becoming the least preferred children of their mothers.

Ultimately, if you had that kind of deep bond with your parents, you undoubtedly saw yourself as a "mom's child" in our society, which means being feminine, which means being poor, inferior in our society. It would be simple, maybe even unintentionally, to blame both the "poor, second-rate" class to which you were subjected and your own class for their aggressions toward you and women. You're trapped in the world of a true no-man. So who do you know, to whom are you entrusting your deepest feelings? Men? Women? Or perhaps no one?

Not wanting to be called a feminine

Aside from being subtly constructed like a friend (not even an HSP trait), imagine an HSM could be viewed as feminine for appearing to be exhibiting, as other women do, intuitive implicit alertness to the risk of physical attack — a caution strengthened by the vulnerability of all HSPs to discomfort. As Gilmartin notes, "pain perception may have an incredibly detrimental effect on the willingness of a man to get along with his same-sex peer group effectively. These concerns will render a male child extremely susceptible to constant bullying, "that is, it makes it as simple as a female, especially a delicate female, to bully.

Or maybe HSMs look feminine because you don't regulate or overtly manipulate others, or because you seem to be a person who shows your feelings— something not accomplished by those who have to be in charge forever.

Perhaps that you seem sadder or more nervous than other guys. Evidence suggests that HSPs with difficult childhoods can exhibit stronger stress and anxiety, as has already been said. That finding is partly attributed to the reality that non-HSMs tend to be remarkably untouched by issues of childhood. The ensuing emotions are experienced by women and HSMs of disturbed infancy.

Maybe non-HSMs are great at managing difficult childhoods because life is smoother for them. Yet others don't even deal well with the pain— they simply push their emotions away. If a mentality I'm-fine-I-don't-need-anyone is used to cover up a profound feeling of inadequacy, it's considered a selfish protection and is used much more by men than women, and much more by non-HSMs than HSMs. Also, HSMs and all women (HSPs or not) respond to their problems with troubling pasts on average.

They get offended, that they are perceived as feminine. Within a man or woman, the problem with a narcissistic protection is that as feelings of anxiety or desire are shut off, one must make confident that such feelings stay ignored by turning off the knowledge of the worries or needs of someone else as well. As a consequence, a narcissist may manipulate others without having to consider the impact on others he or she uses — hardly the type of person in a near partnership that one needs. It's almost as though people with traumatic childhoods are offered a peculiar option of having authoritarian narcissism or not being treated as "true guys." I actually prefer less narcissism than other HSMs want.

Additional Damage to HSWS and HSMS Alike

There are several specific aspects in which gender differences create very common problems in HSWs and HSMs, let's explore them together with all groups.

Foreclosed options

Both HSPs lacking childhood parental encouragement and self-confidence in adulthood appear to be excessively vigilant, refusing prospects out of unnecessary terror. HSWs sometimes pursue refuge in the first profession they find themselves wandering into, or in a political revolution, they are unprepared for, or most commonly, in a precipitous marriage. When within their protected ports, even though the condition is not optimal, they remain put longer. HSW's appear to marry earlier than other people, despite being exceptionally confident and imaginative in high school or college. While, HSMs date and reach their career ambitions later on average than most men, indicating in part their lack of tutoring about how to confidently head out into the world as HSPs.

Low self-esteem

Research indicates that wives frequently have to teach their husbands communication skills, and some husbands who embrace this power have healthier relationships. Yet gaining power requires faith in oneself and the privileges and abilities of your class, which Diane had missed.

For HSMs this same loss of confidence appears to emanate from a failure to comply with the Kid Code. You could have abused it by being so imaginative and "new," laughing or blushing quickly, or not getting distracted by "tough men" things— heat, cold, water in your eyes, itchy skin.

In comparison, both HSWs and HSMs can have difficulty being "sweet," the peculiar cultural ideal. We are often overburdened by stimuli, and we sometimes appear uncomfortable and behave badly in competitive or high-pressure environments, even with a romantic partner we only get to know, rather than appearing pleasant. We can experience anxiety-related symptoms as a consequence of all the discomfort and low self-esteem— a "nervous stomach," rashes, phobias, stuttering, shyness. Such reduced faith and a much more enticing feeling of being.

Poor Boundaries

Both HSPs, whether men or women, are more aware of what other people know, what they want and need. Due to the intense intuitive thinking, you will still sense what's going to happen if people don't have what they need— they will struggle, miss what they intend to achieve, get upset with you, be frustrated at you. And becoming more sensitive, you'll always be annoyed when they sound bad — far more so than most. Therefore, for your own benefit as well as for theirs, you want to want to give others what they desire.

Our community also encourages HSWs, in particular, to respect others— as daughters, brothers, husbands, mates. And that all of a sudden the laws shifted. Remember women might be considered "codependent" and then, as an HSW, you may embrace another excuse to feel ashamed of your natural inclinations.

To HSMs, the problem is that they want "true people" to have overly strict boundaries— to pay little consideration to the needs of others, especially their emotional needs. At the same time, men are supposed to react particularly to women's needs— especially their need to be safe. Perhaps, that is the ultimate paradox. He has to succeed, no matter how exhausted a man is himself. But in what manner? So this is another situation where, as an HSM only wanting to be yourself, you may be suspected not just of being co-dependent but also of being feminine because you are attentive to certain people's emotional needs. If you might be suspected of enabling a woman to manipulate you, whether it is the emotional needs of an individual that you are attending to. Otherwise, you're seen as "not up to" completely meeting all the desires of a woman, still. And if you shut down entirely because of overarousal and confrontation, you're treated as not smart!

Being particularly sensitive to the emotional desires of others, even those of your family, isn't codependency. Codependency happens when you respond to the other's needs in the wrong way. Particularly in the original sense of the term, you will never be considered "codependent" to acknowledge that your buddy is an addict who requires treatment, but only because he or she refuses to address him.

Nonetheless, for some of you, there's something about this codependent word that's valid, and being extremely reactive allows you to build strong boundaries— boundaries that allow in what's helpful and shut out what isn't. Which is not helpful requires the desires of others to react to you in ways that they like, rather than in ways that are beneficial for you all.

Yet when you've been motivated and trained to create strong boundaries, they're actually anything like that. You're not overworked.

Your ego is being taken advantage of. You always say yes, then regret it. If you're moving to the other extreme— now and then, if nearly always — by throwing up barriers that will lock anyone and all out. Finally, you let others convince you that you are frail, nonassertive, and codependent— or else rude, strict, and arrogant— instead of choosing for yourself what kind of individual you are or what rules you want. In brief, all of you are exploiting your sensitivity to impress people very often in attempting to be a "real" man or woman, or moving to the other extreme and embracing the belief that you are vulnerable-until you shut down your sensitivity.

The Highly Sensitive Super person who is at risk

Through being Superman or Superwoman, HSPs compensate for their not becoming the "ideal" guy or woman. And all the companies that they operate with enjoy it.

First of all, given "mega HSWs," we all realize the "ideal" woman is exhibiting great gumption these days. So easy it is for everybody else.

A few people are still working long hours, possibly traveling with their companies, loving success, coping with pressures like soldiers, and fitting in family life as well. It will work out perfectly for nonsensitive, sensation-seeking women. It is about time they shared their temperaments openly. No more sewing and the lengthy dresses.

Yet there are still several HSWs struggling to satisfy those demands. You could have the requisite strong intelligence, faith, skills and abilities.

You may still be strong in the quest for sensations — easily distracted, full of ideas.

And then, you're always the brilliant pioneer in the organization, working the path to the peak, as an HSP too. The sky. A sky. You seem to have the flexibility as well as the endurance they desire. Yet in attempting to fit up with this current Superwoman gender standard, you're undermining who you are and placing your safety at risk.

HSMs could be much more at risk of pretending to be "Super HSMs" as men are far less valued in fast-track jobs than women if they show the desire for personal leisure or extended times with their spouses and families. You will therefore also more likely to be motivated into proving you can work for circles around anyone to prove your manhood and solve your "hidden weakness" invulnerability. So you will definitely dream up fresh ideas using your creativity so creativeness.

For anything but jobs, you have little motivation left and sometimes moan secretly that life is misery, not worth living. With your friend too, it's pretty hellish whether you've got room to get one, or your companion is similarly motivated, in which case the partnership really isn't much. But you're afraid that revealing your fatigue will be a show of insecurity and low motivation that would get around early and potentially lose you your work, and likely the confidence of your wife, relatives, or friends, or so you might imagine. This is my belief that you're normally prevented by your wellbeing, about forty. Adhering to the binary standards of gender may be disastrous.

Good Parents Who Feel Like They Are Bad Ones

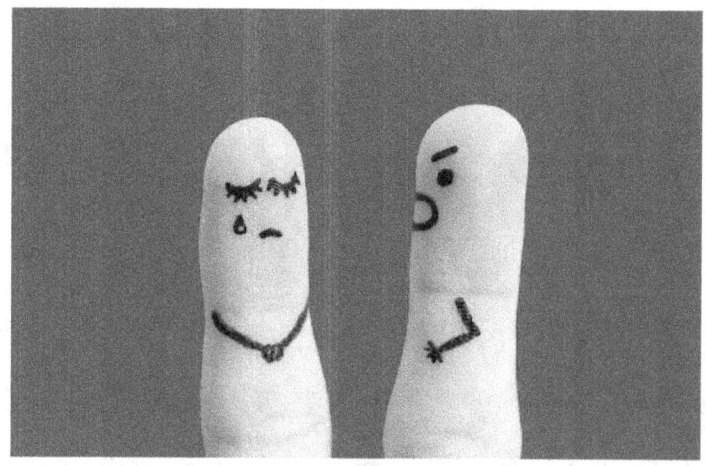

Once I first looked for information on "responsive" or "sensitivity" in the psychology literature, I found just three examples, and two of those claimed that responsive was the only term to identify those that are better at taking care of the children. This skill has nothing to do with whether one is really a mom, but it has more to do with the skill to decipher the hidden signs of a child coupled with an understanding of the experience and helplessness of a baby. Not unexpectedly, after HSWs and HSMs heal from their children's birth such has been seen (each responds strongly), they typically become parents with high sensitivity. Some might not recognize their potential, but most of them are definitely still unconsciously tuned to certain parents.

At the same moment, HSPs may have a clear feeling of being bad at parenting. You know what I think because you're an extremely reactive adult. Sometimes you're irritable, anxious, losing motivation, needing to run married, trying to share your many abilities, or quietly dreaming of how much easier life without children will be. Parenthood is an enormous obligation and stimulation source. It is indescribably painful for both parents to be alert during pregnancy and childbirth, in the best and worst senses, particularly the first. Your body and presence inside feel completely altered. Much of these multiplies after conception, because your kid desperately wants you and too little sleep. You question if you're really going to live. Often, you may worry whether you have made the right choice to have a child. You certainly question whether you are a Successful Mother or a Successful Father often, or even sometimes.

In fact, a conscientious father often feels shut out in the first steps, humiliated and distressed by it, but often profoundly affected by it. So fatherhood holds an additional burden— not only do you aspire to be a nurse so excellent child specialist, but you would also treat the task of shielding and supporting your children financially with considerable severity, no matter how much your wife supports.

Meanwhile, what happens to the mother of your children for your own desire for privacy alone and privacy alone?

The conventional gender roles, now present among both of us, have yet again damaged partnerships with HSPs— this time as guardians. This time the assumptions are about the perfect mother or father— an expectation that no one should fulfill, but no HSP in particular. In non-HSPs, feelings of inadequacy occur mainly in the dreams characteristic of new parents, but in HSPs the feelings seem to be similar and more distressing to the consciousness. I dread to think about the thousands of HSPs who have felt bad for their deep knowledge of the Great Parent and the Terrible Parent hidden so near inside.

Where does sensation-seeking come in?

Before we turn to approaches to these challenges, let's think for a moment about the impact of gender inequality on sensation-seeking HSPs. Sensation finding in this society is obviously a part of the perfect personality. You'll have a bit more confidence if you're a strong sensation seeker (HSS), being more like the perfect man or woman. This is especially true of men, who should be ready for adventure.

Being an HSS will also aid an HSM with love-shyness in particular, encouraging him to make the first move and getting the varied sexual interaction men are expected to do before they settle down.

The downside, of course, is that the HSS / HSP is even more likely to attempt to be superman or superwoman, being powered by both outside powers and these contrasting internal temperamental characteristics. The vulnerable hand gets no assistance until a disease is approved by the patient. A significant caution: You are no less likely to experience fatigue and discomfort as an HSS / HSP. Don't be seduced to try to fill in a gender stereotype that doesn't match you, no matter how close you may be because you're an HSS.

Working on gender troubles

You have now guided through a few dark places. Now let's think about how to put more insight into this. Just as many of the consequences of patriarchy remain surprisingly the same for HSWs and HSMs, so are the strategies to recover, given the generalizations that our society often likes, like "If women feel bad they want to speak about it, but when men feel bad they want to go into their caves and work on projects." Or, "When women have issues they just want to be talked to, however, men want to share and find solutions."

We must all share our feelings and pursue solutions to problems, including those things related to gender. Nonetheless, we are still making the generalities and offer them a bit of their own life. This helps to know the truth and when you want to, you can amend the generalizations. For starters, research shows with a perfect consistency that people are happier in relationships when men and women act in what was historically seen as a "feminine" way in the past— that is, dry, compassionate, emotionally receptive, and happy to address the relationship.

As my anonymous friend claimed, what is referred to as "feminine" is actually "normal human." Luckily, this is also what most people do — against expectations. Recent videotaped studies of newlyweds found that at least these men and women were not at all inconsistent about how much they wanted or helped one another. And the kind of assistance that had been provided by men and women — sympathy and motivation and suggestions — was no different. So much for that sort of stereotype.

HSPs, even less adapted to these generalizations, are in a position to more readily ignore them, which then makes change harder for everyone who already acts in the old ways. We are the founders, transforming culture in a much-needed way. Research shows that those who on average adhere to conventional male-female stereotypes have the least happy marriage and are less open to marital counseling. A large part of this disturbing practice is that the "male rules the roost." There is strong evidence that both parties are less content with such relationships and are more likely to end up divorcing.

Another part of a relationship's "male supremacy" is that the man refuses all demands from a wife woman he can alter. How does a partnership impact the "demand / withdraw pattern?" Withdrawal happens anytime one person tries to speak freely or openly, like making a desire for improvement, and the other fails to communicate, physically turns away, or mentally shuts off. The truth is, although both genders do it, the marriages are deeply strained, divided and likely to end mostly as women claim and men remove.

Christopher Heavey, Christopher Layne, and Andrew Christensen at UCLA videotaped married couples in two conversations to investigate the demand/withdrawal trend— one about something the wife wanted the husband to do better, and one about something the husband wanted the wife to do otherwise. Typical problems were "go out more with me" or "allow me some room to myself." Researchers found that there was no demand/withdrawal during the conversation when the talk was about a shift the husband wanted within the woman. But in the talks men did reject what the wife wanted the husband to change — the men refused to change. The argument of these two cases is that traditional male-dominant partnerships are certainly not indicative of successful relationships. But HSMs that do not feel comfortable dismissing the emotions of others couldn't be on the right track anymore. The only mold people should be trying to fit in the long run, whatever their age, is the one that keeps their partnerships fulfilling and personal.

So, what can you do to heal from the impact of stereotyping discrimination and gender? Okay, just a few suggestions here:

1. Job your self-esteem weak. Reframe the feeling of being inadequate because you are a woman plus an HSP, or because you are not a "real man" because you are an HSP.

2. Develop the standards. Healthy boundaries are versatile, not letting outside in any appeal, nor locking everyone out if you can't trust them or it's not cool to care about.

Discernment is the key here— everyone who approaches you is special, not just a man or a woman or even an HSP or non-HSP, but a person who approaches you at a time when you might or might not be able to respond.

3 Remove the assumptions with real male and female awareness. The only way to reduce the other gender's bizarreness is to listen to members of that elite group and see what they really are like.

Once you know their problems, you will be able to empathize by shifting the attitude from mistrustful to empathy. Even you might be able to help. Of starters, HSMs can go out of their way to give HSWs trust they can be effective in the world, and HSWs can look out for their own assumptions towards "ideal people" and refuse to abide by any traditional views that, for example, are unattractive to a man who sometimes cries or makes long, deliberate choices.

4. For fun, focus on your love-shyness by vowing to see anyone each week. This is a function in partnerships, not of internal work, you'll have to go out and do it. However, along the way, be gentle with yourself. As we have seen, both HSMs and HSWs have reasons to anticipate denial.

Next, determine whether you have deliberately shielded yourself from rejection by staring at or behaving in ways that put you totally out of the race, allowing you to be completely overlooked as a potential date. "Nothing has entered, nothing has been destroyed." I saw many HSPs doing this.

First, it helps to practice a little, to decide what you're going to say before you see someone, and then what else you're going to say if the other looks positive, pessimistic, or hard to read. We HSPs might potentially seem more relaxed if we do some rehearsal — it takes away the squeaks in the speech, the shaking in the hands. You will also have to brace for the eventual rejections, and for the pain of having to leave partnerships that have turned out to be errors.

5. Confront your views on HSMs and homosexuality. In this society, being "feminine" and being homosexual are appallingly misunderstood. Five to ten percent of people are gay, but while I don't have any evidence about it, I'm pretty sure there's no correlation with being an HSM. In a chapter on being "special" in Real Boys, Pollack states that many "tough" people turn out to be homosexuals and that many gentle boys who enjoy peaceful games rather than rough-and-tumble play or contact sports turn out to be heterosexual. For me, gay men have made the same observation— the gay community is as full of macho men as sensitive men, and it is a complete error to presume an HSM to be homosexual. If people take that on board and say the bad, battle that when you can. "Gay, huh? I really wish I was — I love men a lot. "Or," That's an odd idea — I wonder why you felt it was?"

6. Identify what drives you to seek to be so good, to stop being a superman, superwoman or superparent. Are you making up for your "flaw?" At the same moment, trying to please everyone? Refusing to admit you have boundaries? Too enthusiastic about all possibilities of giving up one of them? Once you've accepted the root of this initiative, you'll find it easier to ignore an existence that's too overwhelming to you.

The new attitude may entail the development of new vocations or new ways of guiding, focused on the goal of obtaining the best quality of work or parenting, rather than the amount of time it takes. Your new approach is likely to align self-care with other care in order to maximize both.

(You may do more for the community through role modeling than you do through your actual work.) Meditation is an effective way to achieve equilibrium. Once my son was about three, I began to meditate (Transcendental Meditation, in my case). Only twenty minutes deep inside of myself, especially at night, made all the difference. Dinnertime was turned into a moment of peaceful relaxation from a nerve-shattering experience— with a compassionate mother and child outdoing each other in their overarousal style.

Meditation also greatly assists with function. We've all seen how often ideas come only after time away from the problem.

You will be shocked to see how much more excited you are to be happy or to enjoy after being nothing for some time.

7. Find your gender-responsive trainer. William Pollack and other educators focused on mentoring for youth. Boys will learn more from

being with people beyond their families, men who share their particular interests, to tell them more about how to be in the universe. Thus a vulnerable boy who enjoys reading to soccer, for example, could be mentored by a writer or English instructor who could expose him to the joys of being a man of writing, and who could share stories of his woes as a less than the enthusiastic player. But mentoring may help everyone, especially those with HSPs. And consider in your career a compassionate man or woman or someone who has coped with your present situation and ask if you can meet and share experiences and ask questions. (But for an HSP to accept, you'll need to ensure you're not going to be too demanding— request only one meeting to begin. When one prospective tutor says no, seek another.)

8. Secure yourself from the ones who hate you. I have come to think of the universe as having some places of very thick, strong gender and temperamental discrimination, as I believe in some parts of the military would happen. There are other places where it is so small that it is hardly there at all, as with my own friend, who loves women and loves the type of woman I am, an HSW, very much. I figured it's absolutely essential to shield myself from the dark areas as much as possible.

Because overt showing of bias is not very acceptable these days, it can be difficult to detect. Get to meet enough men and women to be able to sort them properly, as many of them make almost admirable efforts to avoid discrimination, even if they make mistakes at times. What more can you expect if they want to surmount their prejudices? We chose no more to be born into a patriarchal culture than you do.

9. Mind the four races, and then overlook. Earlier in this current chapter, it was mentioned that there would be more space for HSWs and HSMs to be who we are, by getting photos of four genders, not two. As previously described, it seems all animals are supposed to have two breeds— sensitive and not. At least as much as your ethnicity should be of interest to your species. Take a minute to think about your favorite examples of HSWs, HSMs, non-HSWs and non-HSMs (admitting that we don't learn from afar, for sure, who are HSPs and who aren't). To me, maybe "true" HSMs are the U.S. Speakers George Washington, Abraham Lincoln, and Jimmy Carter, along with challenger Robert F. Kennedy and producer Ingmar Bergman, authors Rainer Maria Rilke, Robinson Jeffers, and Stephen Spender, and physician Carl Jung, just for the beginning. Among HSWs are the visionary Teresa de Avila, U.S. First Lady Eleanor Roosevelt, poet

Emily Dickinson, sculptor Camille Claudel, writers Jane Austen and the Brontë sisters, and archeologist Marija Gimbutas (who has done the definitive scientific work on the civilizations of the goddess).

We are all able to provide similarly esteemed lists of "true" non-HSMs and HSWs. Your favorite pioneers, celebrities, adventurers or members of countries or campaigns were probably non-HSMs and all the hard-fighting suffragettes and progressives, including many of the first women doctors, teachers, and scientists, were probably non-HSWs.

Instead, when you're ready to graduate completely from gender stereotypes, consider this: A perfect man or woman is whatever every man or woman is when they act authentically, in harmony with their true self and personality. The identity is no truer concept than you.

10. Use your dreams to heal the hurts of your genders. I also propose that HSPs familiarize themselves with their visions— we imagine beautifully and are well adapted to the introduction of deep personal insight desires. There are three methods of using dreams to cure gender hurts: First, pay attention to the sex of every dream person. It always holds a message about your current gender arrangement or the values that class reflects for you.

In general, if you dream about someone of your own sex, the characteristics of that person are similar to your own, easy to integrate or remember. For examples, when you dream of a certain woman friend of yours who is very extroverted, you know that is a dream of your extroverted self, which is not very complicated to get to. On the other side, when you think of the other type, it usually represents qualities you may never have, or you may not believe. So when you dream of a certain male friend of yours who demonstrates unique assertiveness, stamina, and power, you can realize from that you dream of the kind of strength that you wish to have or need in your life presently, but feel that you can never handle as a woman.

Second, use the dream figure's role to help identify how out of control you are. Suppose, for instance, you and a friend have tried to work through some problem and that night you dream of drowning a young, thin woman. Whether you're a man or a woman, you might want to think back over the conversation of the evening to see if some feminine aspect of you were distracted, washed overboard, drowned, or submerged into the unconscious while thinking, in the traditional sense or as you specifically understand it. By the way, better treatment of your own gendered sections should translate into better treatment of that gender's people.

Second, envision your fantasies of different outcomes that will shift your friendship with the other gender. With this strategy, you do not push a particular end to a vision or idly daydream, but return to a dream with the intention of allowing more to happen in your mind, which in the first instance generated the dream.

In your mind, your more purpose is to take some action, too. This approach will cause useful gender breakthroughs.

In the case of the sinking lady, you could be bringing yourself with her in the water and trying to rescue her. Tell her if she came to sink if she can be rescued. If you had anything to do with it, perhaps you would like to apologize and speak to her. If someone else caused her to drown almost, you can continue by wondering whether that person might constitute a part of you. And if she wanted to kill herself she needed serious help from you— why would she want her future to be taken away? If natural forces swept her away, you may find ways to protect her in the future, and what those forces might symbolize in your waking life.

It is important, in active imagination, that you do not ask any questions or assess what comes to you. Like a vision, the mind will value active imagination as a valuable word. No matter how distressing a picture can initially appear, the purpose is that you should still learn more. The ultimate purpose is kind.

Calming Your Sense and Coping with Pressure

To live in our over-stimulating environment we will constantly implement strategies to relax all five senses — hear, touch, see, taste, and scent. While we cannot function without discomfort we can use specific tools to may each of our senses ' overstimulation.

Calming the Senses

The entire generation hooked to the overstimulation of the sensory organs has now been brought up. As an indication of our modern age's enhanced overstimulation, I've heard several amusement parks are developing full-sensory overload experiences. Current 4-D attractions deliver a frenetic visual experience, buck-and-roll theatre seating, and even the introduction of unusual aromas. A link between elevated stimulus and the larger number of children identified with hyperactive disorders can occur.

The latest panacea for hyperactive youngsters, sadly, is medicating them with powerful drugs that can cause endless side effects. Nevertheless, if these same children lived without electronic devices in a natural world, many of the "hyperactive" children wouldn't need to be medicated.

Hearing

Hearing is potentially the context that provides the HSP with the most difficulties. When you come upon something that triggers unpleasant pain, so you should still shut your eyes. Nonetheless, tuning up deleterious sounds is even tougher. In the emergence of the often omnipresent mobile phones ringing everywhere, noisy music blaring from powerful speakers and honking by furious cars, the poor individual seems to be caught in a clamor cacophony.

The combined impact of these grating noises will trigger severe HSP anxiety.

You might want to play soothing music in the background, at home and at work, to block the noisy noises of new, urban life. From classical to blues, listen to whichever type of music calms you down. If you don't want to hear gentle music in the background, you may want to purchase a white noise machine that helps to block out beautiful sounds by producing a constant, calming rhythm. Loud, intermittent sounds are often covered by a calming fan, air conditioner, or air purifier buzz. An air purifier will soothe the anxiety as it filters air pollutants indoors.

Whenever you're staying in a motel or hotel, turning on the air conditioner or fan will reduce distracting noise from the area. If you don't want to depend on a fan or air conditioner you can also carry a tiny white noise machine with you while you fly. You may also listen to a calming or a directed meditation tape or CD on a daily basis which is very helpful in relaxing the nerves. Most bookstores offer relaxing DVDs and CDs, or for more information, Bringing a headphone with you while you are venturing out into the busy environment is really convenient. You will want to bring a range of calming tapes including controlled therapy, classical music, and other spiritually uplifting effects. Make sure you're bringing extra batteries with you so you don't get lost in a vortex of seismic chaos without a remedy.

Wearing earplugs is another efficient method of than earplugs or raising noise. Many HSPs can consider using earplugs inconvenient, so if you can handle earplugs, masking distracting sounds is a most successful way. Some people favor wax earplugs while some are more relaxed with silicone ones. You that want to wear earmuff-style headphones which construction workers use in extremely noisy circumstances.

Those headphones protect the whole ear and certain HSPs consider them less invasive than adding earplugs. There are also noise-canceling headphones that suppress external sounds by manipulating sound waves. Although such headphones that decrease noises of high frequencies, such as aircraft or refrigerators, they may not seem to decrease noise from speaking more earmuff-style headphones. An audiologist may suit you with a pair of personalized earplugs. Such specifically designed earplugs have the bonus that they can slip comfortably into the ear canal. You should actually shut your eyes and meditate about wearing either earplug, a normal headset, or an earmuff-style headset anytime you just want to hide from the stimuli-saturated environment. You may also use earplugs when listening to your headphones in particularly loud conditions, or use an earmuff-style headphones over earplugs.

Have you ever used a facility for recording? If the studio door is locked, you cannot detect any disturbance from outside. There are sound engineers who will help you build an HSP heaven of harmony and tranquility, soundproofing your home or workplace. You may want to purchase double-paneled windows or thick curtains to block sounds outside. More specifically, the HSP will remain diligent about seeking peaceful places to stay and function. If you live in a loud neighborhood, it's better if your home or workplace faces a dark backyard instead of a busy lane. While flying, ask the hotel or motel clerk often for a private space in the back of the first floor. Don't feel ashamed by the tactics mentioned in this segment, such as using public earplugs or demanding a private space in the hotel. Your primary goal is to deliberately build inner harmony for yourself.

Seeing

The purpose people meditate with their eyes closed is to keep the distractions away from the outside environment, enabling them to delve deeper into the latent calm inside. By continuously experiencing unnecessary stimulation through your pupils, you overwhelm your nervous system directly, which can generate fear which discomfort. Instead of constantly looking at the Television or computer screen, which can over-stimulate the nervous system, consider an eye-opening idea— an eye-closing break from meditation. Only take a few minutes and shut your eyes and observe your breath when seated at home or at work, or just in your parking car. This mini-vacation will leave you feeling more relaxed and ready to tolerate the stimulation better.

This is profoundly calming for HSPs to be able to gaze through a window at a stunning sight in nature. Taking daily breaks during the day to just reflect on your backyard's magnificent oak, the dark green grass of the front lawn, or the crystal-clear azure sky overhead. When you dial in nature's spiritual force, your level of fear will decrease and your level of happiness will increase. You should purchase big pictures or posters of natural environments if your living or work setting is polluted with unnatural, industrial stimuli. Upon staring at a broad shot of a mountain or an ocean photo, you'll feel so much stronger. You may want to purchase wallpaper with a stunning woodland scene that will make you feel like you're living in nature. Fill your home and workplace with plants and flowers to build a healthy and welcoming atmosphere.

Seek each day to invest some time in nature, either walking or sitting in silence. Try to remain concentrated at this moment while you ponder the glorious collection of luscious flowers or the cornucopia of cotton-candy clouds mirrored in a pond's shimmering surface.

You may not know it explicitly, but certain colors are more sedative than others. Surround yourself with soothing colors like brown, gray, green, and other gentle colors. To the nervous system, the shades of the home and workplace will be calming. Bright shades of orange, yellow, and red will over-stimulate, effectively agitating the HSP. Red is linked to rage, and is so appropriately exemplified by the phrase "seeing red." One day, in a brilliant red vehicle, clad in a dazzling red jacket, wearing fiery red lipstick and boasting burning orange eyes, I saw a client of mine pulling up to my office. I always had to bring my shades on and smile at her! The customer told me she didn't understand why she'd just been frustrated and sweaty all the time beneath the shirt. If she stared at her collar's color she may have known what made her feel so angry. You can be drawn to the stuff that can drive you much farther out of control while you're out of reach, so surround yourself with calming colors to establish peace in your life.

Most HSPs are light-sensitive. I found that I have numerous requests to close the blinds while I teach my day students since the strong sunshine can be very disturbing. HSPs may not have to stay in a darkened space, but changing the lighting is crucial so it does not over-stimulate you. Instead of fluorescent, you might want to consider using broad-spectrum lighting to minimize discomfort. It's a smart thing to always wear a pair of shades because you might be having a hard time moving from dark indoor light into the harsh sun.

It is safer for the HSP not to be subject to bright light late at night, because it cannot only conflict with falling asleep but can also cause the nervous system too much stimulus. Nevertheless, introducing oneself to light in the morning after awakening is helpful, and makes the neurotransmitters in the brain know that a fresh day has begun. Even only a tiny amount of light flickering in at night under the bedroom door will interrupt the sleep of a sensitive individual. You should also brush a button at the bottom of the frame, and close all other gaps. Also, you may want to purchase some thick drapes to block off the blinding light from streetlights or a full moon. You should purchase an eye mask which can block the unnecessary light out. Such masks will also help you calm during the day as well as help you get a decent night's sleep.

Touching

Receiving a soothing relaxation is one of the strongest ways an HSP (or non-HSP) can soothe anxiety. Many susceptible people can therefore consider a massage to be too intrusive. This is important for you to give the massage therapist regular suggestions on the degree of discomfort he feels relaxed. Regardless of the signature HSP transparency, the massage therapist's energies will be quickly consumed so make sure to consult the practitioner before committing to a massage.

Because certain HSPs might not feel relaxed being approached by strangers, they might profit more from a companion or good friend having a massage.

In order to have your treatment, you may not even have to go to a salon or body care center. Many retailers also hire massage practitioners, for example, those specialized in fitness items. Now and then you need to take a ten-minute break for a back and shoulder massage. You may want to take a massage class with your friend and swap massages if you can't afford daily massages. Another great choice is to relax yourself and relieve the tension of the day early in the evening.

The only oil that soaks through all seven layers of tissue and intensely calms the nervous system is moist, organic sesame oil. Sesame oil is commonly used in Ayurveda, India's ancient curing method. The compounds of certain oils may have a cooling or heating impact on people according to Ayurveda. Because sesame oil is the most heated oil, don't use it on a hot summer day or when you feel overheated. Consider massaging yourself with the soothing coconut oil while it's humid outside. Don't purchase the toasted Chinese-cooking sesame oil or you'll end up smelling like a wok (which might also strain your nerves). At the nearest health-food shop you can purchase organic sesame seed.

Heat up three to four ounces of the oil and softly and steadily rub yourself across your whole body, from your head to your feet. Let the oil last for about ten minutes on your body, then rinse. Don't place oil on your feet's soles or you could even fall. If you don't want to do a whole-body massage just add some moist sesame oil softly to your forehead and ears. You should also purchase sesame oil, which has been formulated with soothing herbs for true deep healing (see www.oilbath.com for medicated oils). Throughout the evening, add the medicated sesame oil to your forehead and ears and watch the anxiety drift-free.

Warm water for the body is really curative and soothing. Taking a warm bath can be a beautifully soothing treat, particularly when adding a couple of drops of essential lavender oil. Including some sedative natural oils for the nervous system may be profoundly calming. Another successful way to relax the body immediately is to lie in a hot tub with the jets spraying warm water over the stressed muscles for only ten minutes. You may want to buy a showerhead massage for your shower and have fun standing under the calming water.

Make sure you have a nice chair which you can sit on at home and at work.

Some stores sell cushions for the massage which match on your chair. You can purchase a portable wireless stimulation wand too. Many people experience back problems from trying to lie on a bed that is too comfortable or too heavy. Make sure your bed suits your unique physiology and your muscles are comfortable all night long.

Touch itself is rather curative. Evidence shows children impacted are mentally and physically safer than those babies robbed of touch. Ensure sure you receive a lot of kisses every day. Leo Busgalia, the late spiritual leader, used to advise his listeners that everybody wants at least five hugs a day. Have you fulfilled your target today to feast on hugs?

Ammachi, India's spiritual leader, is internationally recognized as the embracing martyr. She tours the globe greeting thousands of strangers every day and has kissed more than twenty million individuals. People queue up for hours to get a hug from Amma, for so soothing is the pure love from her presence.

"Ammachi is the symbol of true devotion, and cures her existence," according to Deepak Chopra. We become immediately uplifted as we are held and nurtured by someone from a position of unconditional affection.

Whether you don't enjoy being closely squeezed or just softly kissed, just don't feel like being hugged. Since HSPs startle quickly, inform your family, families, and acquaintances that with a sudden hug you don't want someone shocking you. One HSP reported that when his wife startles him by embracing him from behind as he washes the dishes it really disturbs him.

Smelling

Most HSP's are odor prone. Several of my students at HSP also indicated that they get nauseated if they are near to someone who has on perfume. When you are prone to certain forms of synthetic odors and you catch yourself seated on a plane or in a theatre next to someone wearing perfume, it is safest to shift your seat instantly. The connection between chemical susceptibility and having an HSP may potentially occur.

When you experience an unpleasant odor response, you ought to be sure the residence is safe from any noxious gases. Often, it is necessary not to operate in a facility permeated with toxic odors. There are lots of natural cleaning items available at the nearest organic food shop that the custodians at the workplace may recommend to use. Buying an air purifier will mitigate the emissions indoors and sanitize the environment. Sometimes, it can block noisy sounds.

Despite rising noise, many individuals in general use masks to prevent inhaling toxic, noxious odors. When you want to wear a mask, make sure you choose a product that is of good quality. For toxic areas a lot of people use masks. For starters, as I toured major cities in India and Mexico, I wore a mask and while some local residents might have assumed it looked odd, I was shielded from noxious odors being inhaled.

One of the advantages of HSPs having a strong sense of scent is their opportunity to use the sensation to help quiet the nervous system down. Aromatherapy is a type of herbal medicine that involves the inhalation of plant and herbal derived essential oils. Many essential oils which are softly scented, such as lavender or rose, maybe successful against tension. Larger health-food retailers will teach you how to use such scents. Yet while aromatherapy may be an ideal way to relaxing the nervous system, it can provide an adverse reaction to certain HSPs. You may want to check the technique before you head out and purchase a potpourri bowl and essential oils, by having a quick whiff of the oils to decide whether this is a good treatment for you.

When you can handle the aromas, you can use lavender, jasmine, and rose, which will change the waves of the brain to establish relaxation and relax. Many organizations are opting to use aromatherapy as management has noticed that soothing fragrances allow workers to function more effectively during the day. You may also smoke any sandalwood or rose incense, which can have a soothing impact on the nervous system. You will also want to recommend purchasing a pillow packed with calming herbs, which encourages relaxing when you inhale as you sleep.

Make sure the ventilation is healthy at home and at college. Check the filters periodically on your air conditioning, heating systems, and air purifiers. If you live in a quiet lane, you may want to unlock your windows to release odors that are old.

Eating and Drinking

Any HSPs are prone to food and drinks, whether hot or cold. In general, it's easier to consume mild beverages and foods than those that pip dry.

Eating warm foods will relax the nervous system as per Ayurveda's healing mechanism (Lad 1984). I had one pupil for many years who had extreme anxiety. He indicated that during the time he felt heightened anxiety she had been on a raw food diet. We found a connection between her fear and her dry, raw diet when we researched her condition. A few months later, she revealed that when she began consuming moist, cooked foods, her anxiety level had significantly decreased.

Another HSP stated that he was really uncomfortable in the winter as he decided to eat only fruit for breakfast. He felt calmer and more balanced as he turned to the hot cereal. You may want to stop consuming ice water, because the cold may be a nervous system shock and lower the digestive energy. Each time you head out to a restaurant to eat, you should ask for ice-free drinks. Drinking iced water will raise anxiety and nervousness on a cold winter day.

Though, it's safe to drink ice water in the summer if you feel overheated and decide to cool down as long as you don't have an adverse reaction (like a headache). Another way to cool off the body is to drink water poured into it with a little lime juice. Occasionally, you might have difficulty consuming frozen products like ice cream. Ice-cold frozen treats will also trigger hallucinations in sensitive individuals, so it's better to gradually let the frozen food melt in your mouth.

Drinking a little warm milk will be a perfect relaxant for you. To flush your toxin system it is important to drink loads of pure water daily.

Drinking a cup of soothing herbal tea, like chamomile, will soothe the nervous system. At a natural food shop, consider buying fresh chamomile and let the herbs simmer in boiling water for five minutes, then strain. This herbal libation is more effective than simply having a bag of chamomile tea. Minimizing caffeine consumption, such as coffee, black tea, and soft beverages may reduce anxiety. Many of my students have managed to gradually rising their caffeine consumption by a systematic process. I consider adding a little extra milk or soy milk in your coffee per day, such that your cup of coffee should just be 25 percent coffee and 75 percent milk in a month. The reduction in caffeine will make you feel more relaxed all day.

Although certain individuals consider alcohol calming, some that are particularly susceptible are potentially experiencing an adverse reaction to just one alcoholic beverage. Also if you believe having a glass of wine at dinner is "no big deal," it is crucial to learn the body's responses to alcohol and to just follow along with the crowd.

The positive thing is that your sense of taste offers you an incredible potential to truly eat tasty foods. The advantage to having an HSP is that the alert taste buds will help you figure out whether a meal is rancid, and you should not be consuming tainted food. One HSP has such a good sense of taste that she was also employed as a taster for wines. Perhaps you will get a slice of chocolate at the work. For a number of men, possessing good taste buds may be called a work like that is a benefit.

Try Taking a Mini-Retreat Twice in One Week

As you are responsive to stimulation and are quickly distracted, it's crucial that you take a mini-vacation at least twice a week to allow yourself a break. Experiencing inner harmony and joy is your birthright. So make sure you clearly put time aside for relaxing. One day of the week, and a couple of hours on the weekend, you should set aside to cultivate yourself. It may immediately feel like a privilege to spend four hours a week relaxing the nervous system, but for the extremely reactive individual, it is a must, in my opinion. You wouldn't think twice about going to the doctor daily to protect your safety if you had a routine specific medical care such as dialysis. Similarly, the mini-retreat is important for HSPs to work in this over-stimulating environment. You'll be nourishing your body, feelings, and spirit during your mini-retreat.

Inform your relatives or fellow members that even if you don't get distracted you require some alone time. When that is not feasible at home, try to locate some spot to have yourself nursed. Will you have a neighbor, sibling or coworker who, throughout the week, will be able to give you their home for a few hours? You might probably agree to feed, clean, or take care of the plants and pets of your "retreat owner" as a swap.

The first phase in building your mini-retreat is to shut off all phones and other electronic devices and make sure you don't get interrupted by any external stimulus, including your household members. If maintaining a quiet setting is impossible, build a noiseless atmosphere by playing some soothing songs, putting on a white noise machine, or using earplugs. Now is the time to just chill in bed or on your sofa and read the book you never seem to get to spiritually uplifting.

When you sound tired when reading takes a relaxing nap with no shame. Place some soothing essential oils in a potpourri bowl or burn any incense if you like aromatherapy. Make a cup of chamomile tea, or your favorite soothing cocktail, if you are hungry. Prepare a special nutritious snack (preferably without sugar), and invest some time truly enjoying every scrumptious morsel you enjoy. Try to shut your head, and concentrate on your tongue's exquisite flavor.

First, seek a spiritually uplifting workout like hatha yoga, or Tai chi. you might want to purchase a DVD or videotape of Yoga or Tai Chi. Another choice is to actually do some gentle relaxing or go on a nature walk. You may want to participate in some of the following after doing any gentle exercise: meditate, listen to a calming track, do incremental massage, pray, read any spiritual upliftment, or compose any blog.

Lastly, you may like to rub the body with warm sesame oil and a nice bath followed. Apply anything you want, from lavender oil to Epsom salts, to the wash. Spend as much time as you want to relax yourself and bathe. Should not set a strict routine to obey but indulge intuitively in the different relaxation strategies mentioned above to settle the nervous system down. You might choose to spend the entire time taking part in only one thing during your mini-retreat.

You deserve to experience daily mini-retreats, so the dates on your schedule for your nursing sessions start penciling right now. Check-in with yourself, though, so you don't start getting frustrated on your calendar by another issue. I always consider having the retreats once or twice a year for longer, whole days or weekends. You should spend some time in a wooded cabin or somewhere you can experience a few days of genuine quiet.

Coping with Time Based Pressure

For an HSP, you'll typically find things difficult while you're under strain from time. Combined with a strong sense of duty, one of the most daunting facets of becoming a highly reactive individual may be to work under time limits. In this segment, you'll learn practical strategies to cope with the everyday challenges of our quick-paced modern society successfully

Creating a Peaceful Work Environment

Living under time constraints with an inconsiderate manager or with hostile bosses is frustrating for the responsive individuals. More than 95 percent of the HSPs surveyed have claimed tension in the workplace influences their physical or mental wellbeing.

Work Stress, Its Public and Personal Costs

Regardless of your sensitivity and the ability to perform the responsibilities at work, you can find yourself frenzied multitasking, performing arduous activities, culminating in physical and emotional burnout. Also in less stressful circumstances, tension will emerge from the ability to be vigilant and not make mistakes. To the HSP, feeling unable to measure up to non-HSP, Type A job expectations can cause disappointment, anxiety, and low self-esteem.

If you operate for a friendly workforce, certain difficult working situations may be changed. A link exists between career satisfaction and successful occupational social experiences. Depersonalization at work is a major cause of both on-the-job tension and unhappiness. The absence of actual personal interaction at work (we are often more inclined to fax the individual in the next cubicle than to get up and speak to them) leads to a workplace sense of anomie.

When you do work that you know is important, the job satisfaction can improve. For starters, once you can appreciate how society profits from your work, you'll actually become more excited about your vocation.

Only HSPs may embrace the belief in our materialistic culture that making more money — even at the expense of your physical, mental, and spiritual well-being — is worthwhile. After you have fulfilled your essential requirements, you may also often push yourself to gain more and more income, assuming that outward remuneration would offer inner satisfaction. Research suggest that, if the essential needs are fulfilled, there is little connection between joy in life and decreased income (Dalai Lama 2003).

HSPs like a lot of rest, and can consider doing a forty-hour week hard to do. Sadly, many American occupations need extra hours for the workers.

Many Americans operate several weeks more than French and German respectively each year. HSPs ought to build their own special job plan, or face getting wrapped up in an exhausting job scenario, despite this out-of-balance American work ethic.

Personal Attitude to Work

Attitude is a significant element in work satisfaction. You will develop a greater respect for your career as you view your job from a global viewpoint. Workers in developed nations and even our own country's workers will do hard physical labor for a fraction of your wage for more than ten hours a day. A number of the unemployed will leap at the chance to work in your profession. Suddenly, the task of being "boring" may sound far more fascinating.

When you are dissatisfied with your job, dig at the source of your discontent. Was that because of the insensitive boss's unfair demands?

Are you disrespectful to colleagues all day long? And is your discontent not happy with certain facets of your life, because of an internal pattern? Generally, we bring our values and behaviors into the workforce and our career represents our existence.

Somewhere else, the subconscious still believes the grass is greener, and the ego thrives on tension to preserve a distinct image.

My dad was one of the only men I met, who enjoyed his work completely. He served as a social educator in the neighborhood, managing local Jewish organizations for more than 50 years. He managed to work as a mentor and supervise pupils in social education long into his late 80s. His passion and positive attitude were two main factors which generated his high level of job satisfaction. And obviously, he was an optimistic and energetic guy beyond the office, taking the mentality to work every day. Another aspect that generated his enthusiasm for his career was his strong interest in supporting others in need, such as the disabled, refugees, and those with physical and emotional difficulties. In a mission he sought particular significance, serving in Europe to reconstruct the Jewish community which was almost devastated by the holocaust.

Also, a boring task gets rewarding and enjoyable as you cultivate a good mindset and collaborate around others who help you. A single man in his early twenties, Derrick works in a factory that exports medical supplies to Asian countries. He noticed that categorizing medical equipment alone was so tedious that in the first week, he would leave the work. During his second week, though, an energetic coworker was allocated, who figured out how each piece of equipment can help a disabled individual recover. The other person made comments as they listened to songs that had raised them. Derrick's whole outlook shifted, and he continued to love his profession so much that several times he happily served overtime.

Although dealing with intense job obligations is harder for a non-HSP, if you acquire the recognition and surrender skills, it can make it simpler for you to perform at work. A postal contractor at one stage was everyday exhausted when he processed letters when a large corporation's CEO said his work wasn't difficult at all. Although a mission was not done the CEO would not care. An HSP student said if she thought she made an error at university, she was incredibly angry. She had agonized about the potential failure for hours.

She gradually started to understand after interacting with her for many weeks that all she was able to achieve was her strongest. Eventually, she let go of the desire to complete accomplish all of the assignments.

I always learned at the first consultation, when I was a career recovery specialist dealing with disabled employees, which people would eventually be rehabilitated into a new workplace. Clients who criticized their boss for their recovery services and worried about their insurance provider also created barriers. When participants had a good outlook towards vocational therapy and acknowledged their disabilities without focusing on their injuries, fresh, rewarding research was usually received.

The stronger the desire to resolve on-the-job challenges, the higher the chance of a successful work experience. Of starters, your job satisfaction improves because you make an attempt to strengthen your interactions with people at work. But if you bring a lot of effort forward to change a tough job condition and nothing happens, you should still leave. You're never really stranded.

More Happiness Even With Less Money

This would improve your sense of well-being to work in a less stressful career that can offer a lower wage but allow you the opportunity to spend more time doing pleasurable and relaxing hobbies (Dalai Lama 2003). No one on their deathbed really wishes they should spend more time earning money at the workplace. Basically, the sum of affection we've expressed for each other is the one and only thing we'll be bringing with us as we exit our bodies.

Materialistic anxieties build a revolving circle. The more income people are creating, the more resources they find they like. The more workers earn ego satisfaction on the job, the more prestige they would seek. People live in expensive, air-conditioned houses tend to commit suicide (Amritaswarupananda 1989). All we just ought to do is air out our brains by questioning whether we'd want to function in a really demanding workplace that hurts our physical, mental and moral well-being.

When you're keeping your work all your life, you're gearing yourself for mental pain as you finally quit the company or withdraw. Live a healthy existence is easier, finding room for a rewarding social life and doing enjoyable things outside the job.

There is a large assortment of work pressure and excitement among HSPs that we can manage. You will find your own equilibrium between dull jobs and one that is too difficult. I know some big phenomenon searching for non-HSPs who excel in a well-paying position at work strain. It offers them a thrill to reach targets for adrenalin, equivalent to a football player scoring a touchdown against a daunting foe. However, the same workplace situation will most definitely cause a severe anxiety response for extremely reactive individuals.

You can often feel trapped in a tough work situation. In fact, the job condition is still changing because you are open to different possibilities. Connie, one of my students, in her 40's, was a female, high-sensation HSP lady. She had served as an administrative assistant with a small business.

Sadly, her supervisor constantly raised her workload and she wound up starting from 8 A.M. six days a week. Around 7 P.M. And either route, driving for an hour. She experienced insomnia and stomach issues owing to excessive work-stress.

Connie thought she wanted the income to afford her big debt payments because no other well-paid employment existed close to her house. Connie told me she had grown up in a trailer and still had a fantasy of staying in a luxurious home. She'd never contemplate going. I suggested that she examine if she could find another position that would be better compensated closer to home. She announced after many weeks of convincing her to search for another career, that she finally found a position near her house working just forty hours a week that compensated about as much as her former sixty-plus hour job a week.

How to Reduce Stress at Work

Many different approaches will help create a work environment that is calmer.

Remember which of these recommendations are German to your workplace in this segment and try to incorporate some of the above concepts into your work situation.

Calming background music can be used to reduce or eliminate ambient noise at work. Most HSPs have told me they also listen to music, wearing a headphone and some have earplugs on the job. Put up inspirational images of natural settings, such as land or seascapes, or pictures of relatives. If you function under fluorescent lights or in an indoor, urban setting, your nerves will be soothed by gazing at nature. If you carry flowers and plants to your office it can also support. Inhaling the sweet scent of roses or gazing at an elegant bouquet can quiet the nervous system down. Surround yourself with happiness by taking in family and friend's videos. Make sure you have a nice chair to sit in and calm your muscles throughout the workday. For your chair, you should purchase a soothing pad that will rub the stress away electronically throughout the day.

Firstly if necessary reduce the number. Let the ringing alert you to calm your body, take a few slow deep breaths and say a phrase like "peace." Don't answer the phone until the third or fourth ring, if necessary. Relax comfortably with those few seconds (Hanh 1991).

Having a daily work plan for every stress is a good idea, rather than rushing into a busy working day every morning automatically. When you first arrive at work, focus yourself on either meditating or doing some steady, intense abdominal breathing for a few moments. Look through the work schedule for the day and agree on a realistic expectation of the tasks to be done, despite the sensitivity. Consider arranging rest periods for some time, and try to perform incremental muscle relaxation at the workstation.

The HSP characteristics of being very conscientious and becoming easily overwhelmed by time pressure will, as we have seen, potentially intensify the tension. When you find the day's expectations are too daunting, consider downscaling the tasks or communicating to your boss. Be rational, and don't build added stress by forcing yourself past your boundaries.

I've learned to say no to take on extra work and personal obligations. While I still feel guilty when I say no, an increased anxiety is the solution for me, as I always know that I need to carry through with any decision I make. Nonetheless, if I know my motivation is high and I have free time, I will often volunteer on-the-spot to help out in ways I didn't want to contribute to earlier. This approach of helping others naturally seems to match the HSP personality by utilizing the sympathy trait without feeling overwhelmed by potential obligations.

Because HSPs are quickly influenced by the moods of other people, you can compose, talk and type faster while you operate with others under time pressure, which exacerbates anxiety. You might want to put a note on your desk that encourages you to operate slowly, rather than being swept away by your coworkers' frenetic moods. They should reassure your peers that Type A workers excel in immediate, productive and aggressive behavior despite their period, not because of it. Then pause to consider the hyper hare defeats the trudging tortoise.

The use of aromatherapy, which is the inhalation of the fragrances of vaporized essential oils, is another successful way of creating occupational quietness.

Some essential oils' scent has proven effective against tension and helps to create relief (Worwood 1997). Research, for example, found that keyboard errors decreased by more than 50 percent when the lemon scent spreads into an office (Worwood 1997).

If you're stuck at work the whole day, exercising or stretching breaks should be taken regularly. The meditation on walking as mentioned in

Chapter 2 can be an effective break. You can always spread, even in your chair when seated.

Continue to do gradual relaxation every hour for a few moments by visualizing all the muscles in your body relaxing further and further while you take a few long, slow breaths. I recall one student worked in a very busy medical office and telling me she didn't have time to take just one rest all day.

However, when seated at her office, she decided to use radical stimulation and found it to be quite effective in reducing tension.

If you have visitors or employees coming to your office, you might want some uplifting magazines accessible to build a peaceful environment. Moreover, serving relaxing herbal tea and nutritious fruit-like treats is another effective way of creating a peaceful work environment.

Many social, large companies sell their workers fitness centers and conference spaces. You might want to explore the possibility of creating a therapy space with your boss. You may find out that the productivity of workers might increase if they had a quiet space during the day to meditate in for short breaks. A peaceful, dark room is a godsend for the HSP operating in a relaxing environment.

To help improve unity at work, recommend installing a suggestion box (Zeff 1999) with your boss. Since the HSP may have many concerns and feel embarrassed to ask for improvements, it would be helpful to have the suggestion box confidential. Also, the suggestion box may give non-HSPs an opportunity to express their view, which may be slightly annoyed by some of the same conditions.

Insomnia-induced HSPs typically find it stressful to be operating early every morning. Ask your employer for getting to work in exchange for taking a shortened lunch hour or going a little later in the day. One student told me he wouldn't have as much trouble falling asleep because he didn't have to be at work early everyday morning. He would remind himself he was always able to sleep the next morning, so it didn't matter if it took some time to fall asleep.

However, if you like going to work early, beginning the day in a peaceful manner with few disruptions can be helpful to HSPs. You have already ended your day peacefully by the time the other workers come. You may then be able to travel home early, before rush hour traffic, and after work have the opportunity to take a nap or take a walk in a park. If you could do some work from home, you will experiment with your manager, which is perfect for the HSP. More and more workers from their home office work part-time or full-time, which really reduces over-stimulation for the HSP.

Note that having successful interpersonal relationships at work is one of the most important factors of job satisfaction. When you are confident, you can have a positive effect on your interpersonal relationships at work. When you feel anxious, the anxiety will escalate between your colleagues. However, the colleagues will also become calmer as you take regular meditation breaks and use other calming methods to create inner-peace. If you maintain a sense of humor and often smile, the feelings of workplace joy and happiness can develop.

Handling Low Self-Esteem and Job Stress

Many people remain trapped in a position that raises their tension as they sincerely believe they deserve it. HSPs who have been informed they are faulty as kids can unwittingly replicate a dysfunctional family at work.

Sometimes in an oppressive work situation, HSPs with low self-esteem may finally feel confident.

Mary, a single HSP woman in her late 50s, worked as a manager for a major corporation for twenty-five years. She told me because of her vulnerability, that she had a traumatic and abusive childhood. She said because of her cruel and inconsiderate employer her career was a living hell. In addition to suffering from anxiety and depression, she experienced heart complications that her doctor described as potentially due to occupational tension. Mary strongly declined, though, to contemplate leaving her work for fear of losing her massive pension.

I advised Maria she may not be around to receive her pension if she continued to work under so much pain. She was able to change things in her life after she joined the counseling and finally realized why she had become used to living in an abusive environment. Finally, Mary left her job and took a position as an instructor at a junior college. Although she had much less pay and benefits, her health improved.

If you want to try a career change there are literally hundreds of attractive, low-stress jobs available. When we're open to new, creative solutions, there are many possibilities in existence.

Creating a New and Stress-free Job

Students also claim they are frustrated with their work, and want to explore a new area. The general advice to be realistic for them when pursuing new career ambitions. If you are employed in a well-paying job, sudden leaving may not be helpful. First, mention your transferable skills, then evaluate whether you adapt your abilities to other vocations. Furthermore, we suggest you consider working in the field you'd like to operate in. Volunteering is an ideal way to gain knowledge that could in turn contribute to a paid job.

One alternative is to start working part-time in a new field and decide if a competitive full-time career is possible for the role to become.

Performing research concerning a new job

Perform a labor market study before embarking on a new line of work.

Ask at least 10 individuals who work in the field you'd like to go into. Speak regarding current levels of recruiting, wages, and credentials, as well as the job's physical and emotional demands. Spend some time looking at the new working climate. It is necessary, as an HSP, to determine objectively whether the role is ideal for a sensitive person. Pay very close attention to the amount of pain, the job environment, and the working hours. As knowledge is usually transmitted gradually by HSPs, it takes a lot of time to perform a labor market survey. Don't overload yourself with too much data or try to take a quick decision.

Working in a field that suits your personality and interests, is significant. You might want to visit a job mentor who can educate you about different career opportunities. Each growing HSP is special. While a high sensation finding HSP in the workplace might love mild relaxation, another HSP will loathe the task. Most HSPs would have trouble working in a position where the hours will constantly change or work the move to the graveyard (11 PM to 7 AM).

Becoming self-employed

To HSPs who don't want to work under the strain of a manager, self-employment can be an excellent option. "Self-employment is a logical route for HSPs," says Elaine Aron. They monitor the hours, the stress, the kinds of people you're working with and there are no problems with bosses or colleagues. "But, she also points out that you have to be vigilant to be a perfectionist to push yourself so far. You also have to be willing to make hard choices. Even, warn of not isolating yourself too much.

If you are operating alone it is important to meet regularly for help with colleagues.

Introverted HSPs could also face several difficulties with the self-employment marketing dimension.

It's necessary to perform a thorough investigation before beginning self-employment as to the viability of performance for your new vocational target. Choosing an area where you do not need to be operating 24/7 is significant. Determine if the product or service you are preparing to deliver is required in your proposed geographic area. You would then be able to complete a survey and assess the number of other people or companies offering the same product or service. Find out what the competition costs and conduct a detailed financial strategy for all facets of the planned company, including cost, overheads, promotions, and salaries. Then you need to figure out how to market your product or service and get updated about all required taxes and licenses. Finally, decide how long it will take you to complete all facets of your work.

CONCLUSION

Thank you for reading all this book!

What do you do when a relative or companion seems to be more fearful of intimacy than you— for example, when there is every sign that you and your partnership are valuable to that other individual, but you're not connected to both?

Obviously, haranguing the other about being more trustworthy doesn't improve. Therefore, the only strategy is to make yourself even more personal, frank and vulnerable — whatever the outcome. That is not an easy task. People who fear trust can be very prickly and critical— it's the best defense, as a cactus would testify. But if you can, be available anyway. Being more independent and different would help enormously so that you feel secure inside yourself no matter what response you get back. In a sense, this way, you have less to risk. Gain the experience above all to know the difference between what you can and cannot change. Yeah, you want to grow and change and ideally so does your spouse. In this, you wish to help one another by encouraging improvement. But one of the biggest steps in development is to embrace one another — to accept the inevitable frustration of the hereditary limitations of your relationship, to understand that each individual is a "package deal" and "when you choose a spouse, you choose a set of problems." It's almost the nature of wisdom to accept the limits of existence and death, to be happy with what you have for as many moments of the day as possible. The chances are slightly better than fifty-fifty that you're happier with your partnership when you're with another HSP than when you are with a non-HSP. It relates especially to HSM's. Those in pairs of HSP / HSP often tend to say they're related to their spouses.

We could also call it good news that so many HSPs have met each other, owing to their greater probability of being introverted, reserved, or just happy to stay home alone on Saturday nights. To make my point, I would add three sets of HSP / HSP by asking them how they met and fell in love. Their tales make you think that there is a powerful cupid or guardian angel entrusted only to the mission of putting together HSPs.

You have already taken a step towards your improvement.

Best wishes!

www.ingramcontent.com/pod-product-compliance
Lightning Source LLC
Chambersburg PA
CBHW070942080526
44589CB00013B/1614